HOW WE TRAVELLED

STEWART ROSS

Wayland

Stewart Ross

STARTING HISTORY

Food We Ate
How We Travelled
Our Family
Our Holidays
Our Schools
Shopping
What We Wore
Where We Lived

Series Editor: Kathryn Smith
Series Designer: Derek Lee

First published in 1991 by
Wayland (Publishers) Ltd
61 Western Road, Hove
East Sussex BN3 1JD

British Library Cataloguing in Publication Data
Ross, Stewart
How We Travelled.—(Starting History)
I. Title   II. Series
388

ISBN 0 7502 0145 2

Typeset by Dorchester Typesetting Group Ltd
Printed and bound in Belgium by Casterman S.A.

Acknowledgements

J. Allan Cash Ltd 16, 20, 24; Bruce
Coleman 8 (Fritz Prenzel), 12 (Roger
Wilmshurst); Mary Evans 25, 29
(bottom); Eye Ubiqitous 4; John
Heinrich 7 (top), 15 (top), 23 (top),
29 (top); Hulton-Deutsch 6, 9, 10,
11, 13, 14, 15 (bottom), 17, 18, 23
(bottom), 27, 28; Peter Roberts 7
(bottom), Topham *cover* 5 , 19, 22;
Wayland Picture Library 21, 26.

Words that appear in **bold** are explained in the glossary on page 31.

Starting History is designed to be used as source material for Key Stage One of the National History Curriculum. The main text and photographs reflect the requirements of AT1 (Understanding history in its setting) and AT3 (Acquiring and evaluating historical information). The personal accounts are intended to introduce different points of view (AT2 – Understanding points of view and interpretations) and suggestions for activities for further research (AT3 – Development of ability to acquire evidence from historical sources) can be found on page 31.

CONTENTS

This family is making a journey by car. Where do you think they are going? Perhaps they are setting out to visit some friends. They might be going to do the shopping.

Every day we see cars all around us, driving along smooth, straight roads. But cars were only invented about 100 years ago. Do you know how people travelled before then?

What sort of road is this? The picture shows the M1 motorway in 1968. Look how little **traffic** there was then.

Motorways are much busier now. Do you know why? When this photograph was taken, people could drive as fast as they wanted. Today people have to wear **seat belts** and there is a **speed limit**. They help to stop nasty accidents.

Have you ever seen a very old car — one that is more than fifty years old? How was it different from a modern car?

This picture was taken in a Morris car factory over sixty years ago. Were your grandparents alive then? Ask them if they remember Morris cars. These cars are not finished yet. Can you see what is missing?

Lucy Chapman is now over seventy years old. In 1924, when she was six, her dad bought his first car. You can see a picture of it below.

'My dad is putting me into the new car for our first trip. He was very proud of it. We were the only family in the street to have a car. We went at thirty miles an hour (forty-eight kilometres an hour). That was very fast then – I was frightened. Then the car had a **puncture** and we had to walk home. I cried when the neighbours laughed at us.'

This girl is riding on her BMX bike. Many people ride bikes for fun. But bicycles are also a cheap way of getting about. Riding is very good exercise and does not cause **pollution**.

Bicycles were invented in the last **century**. One of the first bicycles was the Penny Farthing. It had one huge wheel and one small one. Have you seen a picture of a Penny Farthing?

These **dockers** are going home from work on their bicycles. How can you tell that this is not a modern photograph?

The picture was taken about fifty years ago, just before the **Second World War** began. Few people could afford a car then. Most people travelled by bicycle instead. For longer journeys people used the train.

Where do you think this delivery boy is going on his **tricycle**? Can you guess what is in the box at the back?

The picture was taken in 1932. In those days small bakery shops made their own bread. The fresh loaves were delivered to people's front doors by a boy on a tricycle. Where do we get our bread from today?

In the 1960s some young people used to ride around in gangs. Motorbike riders were known as Rockers. Those who rode scooters were known as Mods. Sometimes the Mods and Rockers had fights.

Does this picture show Mods or Rockers? These days everyone who rides a scooter or motorbike has to wear a helmet.

RAILWAYS

Can you see the old steam-engine in this picture? This railway line is not used any more. Flowers have grown over the tracks.

Railway lines used to run all over the country – even to small villages. Most people travel by car today, so many railway stations have closed down.

Have you ever seen a steam-engine like this one? Until about thirty years ago, most trains looked like the one in this picture.

Steam-engines were very exciting to watch, but they caused a lot of pollution. Look at the dirty smoke in the photograph.

Perhaps your parents or grandparents remember travelling on a train like this one. The picture was taken in 1948. It shows the first **diesel** engine which British Railways bought.

British Railways wanted to make trains more modern. They hoped that people would travel by rail rather than by car. But people still do not use the railways very much. Can you think of any reasons why?

Bill Rawlins used to work on the railways. He was a fireman on a steam engine. It was his job to put coal on to the fire. The fire made the steam which drove the engine of the train.

'There were two of us in the cab – the driver and myself. His job was easier than mine. He turned the wheels and pulled all the levers. My work was really hard. I shovelled tonnes of coal on to the fire. When I finished work I was covered in dirt from head to foot.'

Have you been on a long journey in a large coach? These coaches are picking up their passengers at Dover harbour.

Modern coaches are comfortable and fast. Some of the big ones even have toilets at the back. Buses and coaches are cheap, and take passengers exactly where they want to go. Do you prefer buses or trains?

How much does it cost you to travel on a bus? Forty years ago most rides cost only a penny or two.

These children are getting on to a bus to go into town. The picture was taken in 1952. How is this bus different from the ones you have travelled on? Ask your grandparents about buses in the 1950s.

This picture shows a trolley bus in 1923. Trolley buses worked on electricity. Can you see the long poles on the roof? These carried the electricity from the wires above the street to the bus. The bus used this power to move.

The driver had to be careful to follow the wires. If the poles became unhooked, the bus stopped in the middle of the road.

This photograph shows two London trams in 1936. Trams were a clean and easy way to travel in towns and cities. They ran through the streets on rails, like trains. Trams also used electricity to move, like trolley buses.

Some big towns are building new tram lines. They want people to use them instead of cars. Can you think why?

Here is a hovercraft leaving Dover harbour. It is a quick and modern way to cross the **Channel**. Before hovercraft were invented, people used boats or aeroplanes to travel to France.

Now it is also possible to travel to France underneath the sea, using the Channel Tunnel. The tunnel was dug beneath the seabed. Trains run through the tunnel, carrying passengers and cars.

This family is enjoying a trip on a **barge**. Can you spot the name of the boat? Barges travel on rivers and **canals**. They used to be pulled by horses.

Barges were built many years ago to carry heavy loads. The people who sailed them lived in cabins at the back of the boat. But barges travel very slowly. Today we use lorries and trains to transport heavy things quickly.

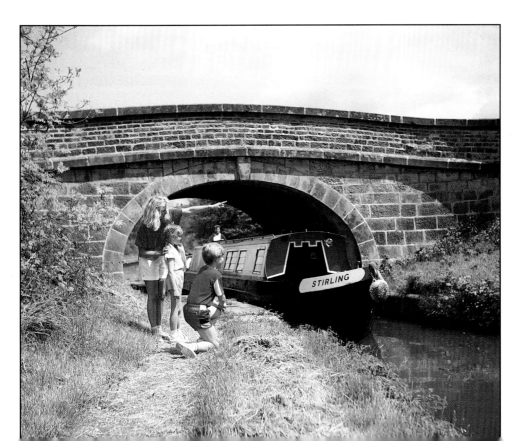

How do you think that people used to travel to far-away countries? Here is the England cricket team setting off for Australia in 1932.

The team are going by passenger **liner**. This was the normal way to reach far-away countries then. The journey took many weeks. It was very comfortable and in those days much safer than flying.

Daisy Collins was very lucky. Her dad took the family on a trip to the USA in 1938. They travelled on a huge liner called the Queen Elizabeth.

'The ship was wonderful. It was like a floating hotel. The **crew** were very kind to me. But they gave me so many sticky sweets that I was sick. Mum got a bit cross. She asked the men not to spoil me.'

Have you ever walked further than a kilometre? These children are going on a walk of twenty-four kilometres to collect money for a hospital. Most of them have never walked so far before.

At the beginning of this century people walked much more than they do today. But they did not do it for fun. There were few cars and no buses. Walking was often the only way of travelling.

This picture shows different ways of travelling. Can you see the motor car and the bicycle, as well as the horse and cart?

For hundreds of years horses were used for riding and pulling carts. When trains, cars and lorries were invented, horses were not needed for transport any more. We usually keep horses for pleasure now.

INTO THE AIR

Have you flown in an aeroplane? These passengers have just landed after a long flight in a jet aeroplane. Millions of people fly all over the world every year.

Flying is quite a new way of travelling. The first aeroplane flew in 1903. That was about ninety years ago. Since then planes have been made much bigger, faster and safer.

How is this aeroplane different from a modern one? Look at the wings, tail and engines. Passenger aeroplanes like this were used in the 1930s. Were your parents alive then?

These planes could not fly very high. They could only carry a few passengers, so tickets were expensive. In bad weather they had to stay on the ground.

This large passenger aeroplane was popular in the 1950s and the 1960s. Travelling by air was becoming much cheaper then. Many people flew for the first time.

How many of your friends and family have flown in an aeroplane? See if you can find someone who flew in the 1950s. Ask them what flying was like then.

John Miller was the captain of a flying boat in the 1930s. You can see his aeroplane in the picture on this page. It could take off from water and from land.

'In those days flying was a real adventure. We could not always tell where we were going in the clouds. When it was stormy we could not land on the sea to pick up passengers. But flying boats were wonderful planes.'

Talking to people

Ask grown-ups you know well about how they travelled when they were young. They probably have some good stories to tell, and they may have some interesting old photographs.

Using your eyes

Look in old books, papers and magazines to find out how people used to travel. If you watch old films carefully they will show you many kinds of cars, trains, boats and aeroplanes from the past. You can see real ones in transport museums.

Transport on display

Why not make a scrapbook or a display about how people travelled in the past? You could do some drawings of old cars, trains and buses that you have seen. Try to make a collection of old objects to do with travel, such as tickets.

Read all about it

The pictures from these books will help you find out more about how people travelled in the past:

Lets Look At Series: Wayland, 1988/89
Time and Motion: John Cockcroft, Collins, 1987
Timelines Series: Franklin Watts, 1991
Transport in History: A. Blackwood, Wayland, 1984

Barge   A boat which carries goods on a canal or river.

Canal   A river made by people.

Century   One hundred years. We live in the twentieth century, which began in 1901. It will end in 2000.

Channel   The sea between England and France.

Crew   The people who work on a ship or an aeroplane.

Diesel   A powerful kind of motor. It is used in lorries, railway engines and in some cars.

Dockers   People who load and unload ships.

Liner   A large passenger ship.

Pollution   Dirt or rubbish which harms the Earth.

Puncture   A hole in a tyre which lets the air out.

Seat belts   A safety belt which can be fastened to hold a person in their seat in a car or plane.

Second World War   The war that lasted from 1939 to 1945. The fighting spread all around the world.

Speed limit   A rule which tells us the highest speed we can drive at on a road.

Traffic   All the cars, lorries, vans and cycles moving on a road.

Tricycle   A cycle with three wheels.

INDEX